Blundell Surname

Ireland: 1600s to 1900s

From Ireland Church Records of Baptism, Marriage and Death

Comprised of Roman Catholic and Church of Ireland Records

From Counties Carlow, Cork, Kerry and Dublin City

Compiled by **Donovan Hurst**

November 14, 2012

ISBN: 0985696834
ISBN-13: 978-0-9856968-3-2

Dedication

This work is dedicated to all of those that came before us and shaped our lives to make us the people that we are today.

Table of Contents

Introduction

This is a compilation of individuals who have the surname of Blundell that lived in the country of Ireland from the 1600s to the 1900s. I have placed each entry into one of four categories: Families, Individual Births/Baptisms, Individual Burials, and Individual Marriages. If a marriage entry primarily concerns an Individual Blundell whom is female, then I have placed that entry under the category of Individual Marriages. If a marriage entry primarily concerns an Individual Blundell whom is male, then I have placed that entry under the category of Families. Images of many of these listings are available at http://churchrecords.irishgenealogy.ie/churchrecords/.

To help guide the reader of this work, the format of this book is as follows:

- Main Family Entry (Husband and Wife) (Father and Mother)

  o Child of Main Family Entry, including Spouse(s) when available

    ▪ Grandchild of Main Family Entry, including Spouse(s) when available

      • Great-Grandchild of Main Family Entry, including Spouse(s) when available

(**Bolded Text**) following any entry includes any additional information such as Residence(s), Occupation(s), Signature(s), etc. when available.

i

Hurst

Some of the fonts used in this work symbolizes Celtic writing. The traditional letters, numbers, and punctuation marks and their Celtic counterparts are as follows:

Traditional Letters (Uppercase & Lowercase)

A a B b C c D d E f G g H h I i J j K k L l M m N n O o P p Q q R r S s T t U u V v W w X x Y y Z z

Celtic Letters (Uppercase & Lowercase)

A a B b C c D ð E e F f G g H h I í J j K k L l M m

N n O o P p Q q R ʀ S s T t U u V ʋ W ʍ X x Y ʒ Z z

Traditional Numbers

1 2 3 4 5 6 7 8 9 10

Celtic Numbers

1 2 3 4 5 6 7 8 9 10

Traditional Punctuation

. , : ' " & - ( )

Celtic Punctuation

. , : ' " & - ( )

Parish Churches
Cork & Ross
(Roman Catholic or RC)

Kinsale Parish.

Dublin (Church of Ireland)

Arbour Hill Barracks Parish, Glasnevin Parish, Grangegorman Parish, Portobello Barracks Park Parish, Rathmines Parish, Rotunda Chapel Parish, St. Audoen Parish, St. Bride Parish, St. Catherine Parish, St. George Parish, St. James Parish, St. John Parish, St. Kevin Parish, St. Luke Parish, St. Mark Parish, St. Mary Parish, St. Michan Parish, St. Nicholas Without Parish, St. Patrick Parish, St. Paul Parish, St. Peter Parish, St. Stephen Parish, and St. Werburgh Parish.

Dublin (Roman Catholic or RC)

SS. Michael & John Parish, St. Andrew Parish, St. Mary, Pro Cathedral Parish, St. Michan Parish, and St. Nicholas Parish.

Kerry (Church of Ireland)

Ballymacelligott & Ballyseedy Parish, Dingle Parish, Killehenney Parish, Listowel Parish, and Tralee Parish.

Blundell Surname Ireland: 1600s to 1900s

Families

- Andrew Blundell & Catherine Blundell

  - Sarah Blundell – bapt. Jul 1825 (Baptism, **St. Nicholas Parish (RC)**)

  - Catherine Blundell & James Darcy – 25 Feb 1868 (Marriage, **St. Mary, Pro Cathedral Parish (RC)**)

    - James Darcy – b. 9 Feb 1868, bapt. 28 Feb 1868 (Baptism, **St. Mary, Pro Cathedral Parish (RC)**)

Catherine Blundell (daughter):

Residence - 3 Nerney's Court - February 25, 1868

February 28, 1868

James Darcy, son of James Darcy & Marcella Darcy (son-in-law):

Residence - 38 Upper Baggot Street - February 25, 1868

- Andrew Blundell & Mary A. Gill

  - Andrew Blundell – bapt. 11 Dec 1835 (Baptism, **St. Nicholas Parish (RC)**)

  - James Blundell – bapt. 20 Jun 1838 (Baptism, **St. Nicholas Parish (RC)**)

  - Teresa Blundell – bapt. 12 Jan 1841 (Baptism, **SS. Michael & John Parish (RC)**)

  - Elizabeth Teresa Blundell – bapt. 27 Oct 1845 (Baptism, **SS. Michael & John Parish (RC)**)

- Andrew Blundell & Mary Anne Lynch

  - Anne Blundell – bapt. 18 Aug 1834 (Baptism, **St. Nicholas Parish (RC)**)

1

- Andrew Blundell & Unknown

  o Richard Blundell & Catherine Wade – 4 May 1846 (Marriage, St. Catherine Parish)

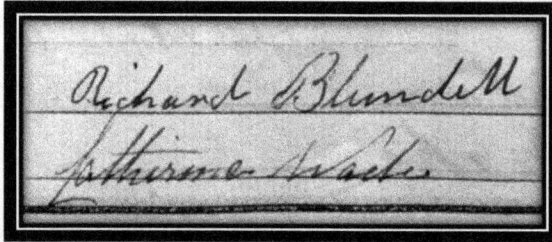

Signatures:

Richard Blundell (son):

    Residence - Love Lane - May 4, 1846

    Occupation - Printer - May 4, 1846

Catherine Wade, daughter of Joseph Wade & Unknown (daughter-in-law):

    Residence - Love Lane - May 4, 1846

Joseph Wade (father):

    Occupation - Watch Maker

Andrew Blundell (father):

    Occupation - Printer

Blundell Surname Ireland: 1600s to 1900s

Wedding Witnesses:

M. Buly & Thomas Hunt

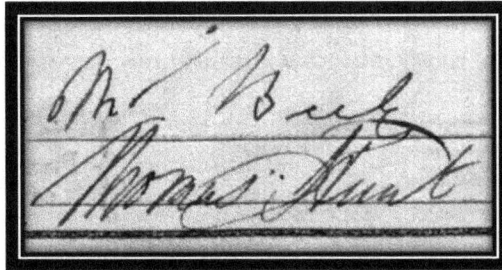

Signatures:

- Charles Blundell & Rose Unknown

    o Norah Anne Blundell – b. 31 Jan 1899, bapt. 19 Feb 1899 (Baptism, **St. Kevin Parish**)

Charles Blundell (father):

Residence - 29 Ovoca Road, South Circular Road - February 19, 1899

Occupation - Furniture Salesman - February 19, 1899

- Daniel Blundell & Mary Blundell

    o Elizabeth Sibela Blundell – bapt. 21 Jul 1695 (Baptism, **St. Michan Parish**)

    o Ralph Blundell – bapt. 22 Nov 1696 (Baptism, **St. Michan Parish**)

    o Dorothy Blundell – bapt. 22 Jun 1699 (Baptism, **St. Michan Parish**)

Daniel Blundell (father):

Occupation - Merchant - July 21, 1695

November 22, 1696

Gentleman - June 22, 1699

Hurst

- Edward Blundell & Jane Doyle

  o John Blundell – bapt. 17 Jan 1806 (Baptism, **St. Michan Parish (RC)**)

- Edward Blundell & Mary Blundell

  o John Edward Blundell – bapt. 15 Feb 1852 (Baptism, **Arbour Hill Barracks Parish**)

Edward Blundell (father):

Residence - Linen Hall - February 15, 1852

Occupation - Private 39th - February 15, 1852

- Francis Blundell & Susan Unknown

  o Judith Blundell – bapt. 4 Feb 1750 (Baptism, **St. Audoen Parish**)

  o Susan Blundell – bapt. 24 Sep 1751 (Baptism, **St. Audoen Parish**)

  o John Blundell – bapt. 9 Mar 1754 (Baptism, **St. Audoen Parish**)

- Francis Blundell & Ursula Davis, bur. 23 May 1673 (Burial, **St. Audoen Parish**) – 29 Dec 1670 (Marriage, **St. Bride Parish**)

Ursula Davis, daughter of Paul Davis.

- Francis Blundell & Unknown

  o George Knight Blundell – bapt. 15 Nov 1676 (Baptism, **St. Peter Parish**)

  o William Blundell – bapt. 18 May 1683 (Baptism, **St. Peter Parish**)

  o Charles Blundell – bapt. 17 Jan 1684 (Baptism, **St. Peter Parish**)

- George Blundell & Anne Unknown

  o George Blundell – bapt. 17 Jan 1775 (Baptism, **St. Mary, Pro Cathedral Parish (RC)**)

Blundell Surname Ireland: 1600s to 1900s

- George Blundell & Jane Fagan

  o Henry Francis Blundell – b. 2 Aug 1860, bapt. 6 Aug 1860 (Baptism, **St. Michan Parish (RC)**)

  o Emily Blundell & William Scott – 14 Aug 1895 (Marriage, **St. Mary, Pro Cathedral Parish (RC)**)

     ▪ William Michael Scott – b. 10 Sep 1897, bapt. 20 Sep 1897 (Baptism, **St. Mary, Pro Cathedral Parish (RC)**)

Emily Blundell (daughter):

　Residence - 16 Cumberland Street - August 14, 1895

William Scott, son of John Scott & Mary Shea (son-in-law):

　Residence - 16 Cumberland Street - August 14, 1895

　　　2 Mountjoy Court - September 20, 1897

  o Andrew Blundell, b. 5 May 1866, bapt. 18 May 1866 (Baptism, **St. Mary, Pro Cathedral Parish (RC)**) & Elizabeth Myler – 4 Jul 1897 (Marriage, **St. Mary, Pro Cathedral Parish (RC)**)

     ▪ Sarah Blundell – b. 2 Jul 1898, bapt. 13 Jul 1898 (Baptism, **St. Mary, Pro Cathedral Parish (RC)**)

Andrew Blundell (son):

　Residence - 14 Grenville Street - July 4, 1897

　　　26 Upper Gardiner Street - July 13, 1898

Elizabeth Myler, daughter of Charles Myler & Sarah Barry (daughter-in-law):

　Residence 6 Gardiner's Lane - July 4, 1897

- James Joseph Blundell – b. 15 Apr 1870, bapt. 2 May 1870 (Baptism, **St. Mary, Pro Cathedral Parish (RC)**)
- Amelia Jane Blundell – b. 9 Sep 1873, bapt. 15 Sep 1873 (Baptism, **St. Mary, Pro Cathedral Parish (RC)**)

George Blundell (father):

Residence - 139 Dorset Street - August 6, 1860

41 Dorset Street - May 18, 1866

38 Upper Dorset Street - May 2, 1870

38 Dorset Street - September 15, 1873

- Henry Blundell & Amelia Eakins
  - Henry Richard Blundell – bapt. 15 Mar 1829 (Baptism, **St. Paul Parish**)
  - Robert Blundell, bapt. 29 May 1837 (Baptism, **St. Mary, Pro Cathedral Parish (RC)**) & Julia Kane – 24 Feb 1862 (Marriage, **St. Mary, Pro Cathedral Parish (RC)**)
    - Amelia Blundell – b. 2 Jan 1863, bapt. 12 Jan 1863 (Baptism, **St. Mary, Pro Cathedral Parish (RC)**)
    - Mary Teresa Blundell – bapt. 9 Apr 1844 (Baptism, **St. Michan Parish (RC)**)
    - Gulielmo Blundell – b. 25 Nov 1864, bapt. 5 Dec 1864 (Baptism, **St. Mary, Pro Cathedral Parish (RC)**)

Robert Blundell (son):

Residence - 76 Capel Street - February 24, 1862

33 Lower Liffey Street - January 12, 1863

Blundell Surname Ireland: 1600s to 1900s

December 5, 1864

Julia Kane, daughter of Gulielmo Kane & Jean Kane (daughter-in-law):

Residence - 2 Lower Jervis Street, Super 8 Christ Church Place -

February 24, 1862

- o William Blundell – bapt. 18 Jun 1839 (Baptism, **St. Michan Parish** (RC))
- o Esther Blundell & James McKeon – 5 Nov 1874 (Marriage, **St. Mary, Pro Cathedral Parish** (RC))

Esther Blundell (daughter):

Residence - 76 Capel Street - November 5, 1874

James McKeon, son of Patrick McKeon & Bridget Unknown (son-in-law):

Residence - Gibraltar Villa Dolphin's Barn - November 5, 1874

- Henry Blundell & Elizabeth Jane Ellen Blundell
  - o Thomas Henry Blundell – b. 5 Jan 1844, bapt. 24 Mar 1844 (Baptism, **St. George Parish**)
  - o Thomas William Blundell – b. 22 Apr 1845, bapt. 18 Jun 1845 (Baptism, **St. George Parish**)

Henry Blundell (father):

Residence - No. 1 Washington Place - March 24, 1844

No. 1 Washington Place Royal Canal - June 18, 1845

Occupation - Gentleman - March 24, 1844

June 18, 1845

Hurst

- Henry Blundell & Elizabeth Ellen Blundell

  o Lewis Proctor Blundell – b. 25 Nov 1849, bapt. 9 Dec 1849 (Baptism, St. Mary Parish)

  o Amelia Caroline Blundell – b. 26 Feb 1853, bapt. 1 May 1853 (Baptism, Grangegorman Parish)

Henry Blundell (father):

Residence - 33 Jervis Street - December 9, 1849

35 Phibsboro Road - May 1, 1853

Occupation - Printer - December 9, 1849

Compositor - May 1, 1853

- Henry Blundell & Ellen Blundell

  o Richard Blundell – b. 29 Jun 1856, bapt. 12 Jul 1856 (Baptism, St. Peter Parish)

Henry Blundell (father):

Residence - No. 37 Lower Clanbrone Street - July 12, 1856

Occupation - Overseer Every Mail - July 12, 1856

- Henry Blundell & Mary Anne Blundell

  o Henrietta Blundell – bapt. 15 Nov 1797 (Baptism, St. Mary Parish)

- James Blundell & Mary Unknown

  o George Blundell – bapt. 26 Mar 1788 (Baptism, St. Nicholas Parish (RC))

- James Blundell & Unknown

  o Sophia Blundell – bapt. 29 Aug 1621 (Baptism, St. John Parish)

Blundell Surname Ireland: 1600s to 1900s

- John Blundell & Ellen Knowd – 22 Aug 1848 (Marriage, **St. Andrew Parish** (RC))

  - Mary Anne Blundell – b. 1850, bapt. 1850 (Baptism, **St. Andrew Parish** (RC))

  - John Blundell – bapt. 1852 (Baptism, **St. Andrew Parish** (RC))

  - Mary Blundell – bapt. 1853 (Baptism, **St. Andrew Parish** (RC))

  - Rachel Blundell – bapt. 1854 (Baptism, **St. Andrew Parish** (RC))

  - Patrick Blundell – b. 1856, bapt. 1856 (Baptism, **St. Andrew Parish** (RC))

  - Thomas Blundell – b. 1857, bapt. 1857 (Baptism, **St. Andrew Parish** (RC))

  - Mary Anne Blundell – b. 1858, bapt. 1858 (Baptism, **St. Andrew Parish** (RC))

John Blundell (father):

Residence - 2 City Quay - 1858

- John Blundell & Jane Adams – 30 Nov 1814 (Marriage, **St. Mary Parish**)

Jane Adams (wife):

Relationship Status at Marriage - widow

- John Blundell & Jane Lucy

  - William Percival Blundell – b. 6 Feb 1891, bapt. 9 Feb 1891 (Baptism, **St. Mary, Pro Cathedral Parish** (RC))

John Blundell (father):

Residence - 84 Great Britain Street - February 9, 1891

Hurst

- John Blundell & Magaret Mahoney

  - Teresa Blundell & John Martin – 30 Jan 1859 (Marriage, **St. Mary, Pro Cathedral Parish (RC)**)

    - John Michael Martin – b. 29 Oct 1859, bapt. 9 Nov 1859 (Baptism, **St. Michan Parish (RC)**)

Teresa Blundell (daughter):

Residence - 10 Bolton Street - January 30, 1859

John Martin, son of John Martin & Margaret Martin (son-in-law):

Residence - 10 Bolton Street - January 30, 1859

No. 2 Dominick Street - November 9, 1859

- John Blundell & Mary Blundell

  - Mary Blundell – bapt. 16 May 1814 (Baptism, **St. Mary Parish**)

- John Blundell & Mary Flood

  - Michael Blundell – bapt. 30 Sep 1841 (Baptism, **St. Michan Parish (RC)**)

- John Blundell & Mary Elizabeth Blundell

  - Martha Blundell – b. 7 Jan 1865, bapt. 17 Jan 1865 (Baptism, **St. Luke Parish**)

John Blundell (father):

Residence - 13 Montague Street - January 17, 1865

Occupation - Organ Builder - January 17, 1865

- John Blundell & Unknown

  - Isabel Blundell – bapt. 2 Sep 1652 (Baptism, **St. John Parish**)

Blundell Surname Ireland: 1600s to 1900s

- John Blundell & Unknown

  o William Blundell (1st Marriage) & Mary Troy, d. bef. 5 Jul 1868 – 15 Mar 1859 (Marriage, **St. Michan Parish**)

Signatures:

  o William Blundell (2nd Marriage) & Mary Anne Connor – 5 Jul 1868 (Marriage, **St. Michan Parish**)

Signatures:

  ▪ Mary Blundell & John Crichton – 26 Dec 1885 (Marriage, **St. Werburgh Parish**)

Signatures:

11

Hurst

Mary Blundell (daughter):

    Residence - 16 Essex Quay - December 26, 1885

    Relationship Status at Marriage - minor age

John Crichton, son of Archibald Crichton & Unknown (son-in-law):

    Residence - 22 Lower Exchange Street - December 26, 1885

    Occupation - Gunsmith - December 26, 1885

Archibald Crichton (father):

    Occupation - Watchmaker

William Blundell (father):

    Occupation - Boot & Shoe Manufacturer

Wedding Witnesses:

George James Franklin & Prudence Boucher

Signatures:

Blundell Surname Ireland: 1600s to 1900s

- Sarah Blundell – b. 28 Apr 1868, bapt. 6 May 1868 (Baptism, **Rotunda Chapel Parish**)

  (Baptism, **St. Mary Parish**)

- Teresa Elizabeth Blundell – b. 12 Aug 1870, bapt. 11 Sep 1870 (Baptism, **St. John Parish**)

- Henry Blundell – b. 17 Nov 1872, bapt. 1 Dec 1872 (Baptism, **St. John Parish**)

- John Joseph Blundell – b. 21 Mar 1874, bapt. 7 Jun 1874 (Baptism, **St. John Parish**)

- William Thomas Blundell – b. 14 Nov 1875, bapt. 26 Mar 1876 (Baptism, **St. John Parish**)

- Margaret Ellen Blundell – b. 22 Jul 1878, bapt. 18 Sep 1878 (Baptism, **St. Werburgh Parish**)

- Albert Blundell – b. 9 Feb 1881, bapt. 30 Mar 1881 (Baptism, **St. Werburgh Parish**)

William Blundell (father):

Residence - 3 Mountrath Street - March 15, 1859

July 5, 1868

May 6, 1868

7 Wood Quay - September 11, 1870

17 Wood Quay - December 1, 1872

June 7, 1874

16 Essex Quay - March 26, 1876

September 18, 1878

March 30, 1881

Occupation - Shoe Maker - March 15, 1859

May 6, 1868

September 11, 1870

Hurst

December 1, 1872

March 26, 1876

September 18, 1878

Boot Maker - July 5, 1868

June 7, 1874

March 30, 1881

Boot & Shoe Manufacturer

Relationship Status at 1st Marriage - minor

Relationship Status at 2nd Marriage - widow

Mary Troy (1st wife), daughter of James Troy & Unknown (daughter-in-law):

   Residence - 4 Mountrath Street - March 15, 1859

   Occupation - Boot Closer - March 15, 1859

James Troy (father):

   Occupation - Architect

Wedding Witnesses (1st Marriage):

Mary Ann Unknown & James Brady

Signatures:

Blundell Surname Ireland: 1600s to 1900s

Mary Anne Connor (2nd wife), daughter of William Connor & Unknown

(daughter-in-law):

Residence - 24 Old Kilmainham - July 5, 1868

William Connor (father):

Occupation - Coach Builder

Wedding Witnesses (2nd Marriage):

James Parks & Elizabeth Parks

Signatures:

John Blundell (father):

Occupation - Officer in Four Courts

Crier of the Rolls Court

- John William Blundell & Mary Blundell
  - o Thomas Blundell – b. 4 May 1896, bapt. 20 May 1896 (Baptism, **St. Mark Parish**)

John William Blundell (father):

Residence - 126 Great Brunswick Street - May 20, 1896

Occupation - Paver - May 20, 1896

- Joseph Blundell & Anne Thomas – 8 Jul 1820 (Marriage, **St. Werburgh Parish**)

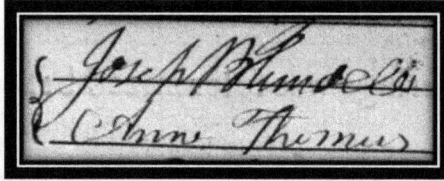

Signatures:

- o Elizabeth Blundell – b. 10 Sep 1821, bapt. 16 Sep 1821 (Baptism, **St. Mary Parish**)

- o Anne Blundell – b. 1 Oct 1824, bapt. 10 Oct 1824 (Baptism, **St. Mary Parish**)

- o Mary Blundell – b. 21 Feb 1826, bapt. 1 Mar 1826 (Baptism, **St. Mary Parish**)

- o Joseph Lewis Blundell – bapt. 11 Jun 1830 (Baptism, **St. Mary Parish**)

Joseph Blundell (father):

Residence - 187 Britain Street - June 11, 1830

Occupation - Printer - June 11, 1830

Wedding Witnesses:

Richard Smallman & Lewis Thomas

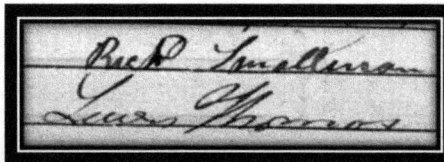

Signatures:

- Joseph Blundell & Elizabeth Bunn – 1 Jun 1705 (Marriage, **St. Michan Parish**)

Joseph Blundell (husband):

Residence - Clockmaker - June 1, 1705

Blundell Surname Ireland: 1600s to 1900s

- Joseph Blundell & Mary Gorman (G o r m a n)

  o Joseph James Blundell – b. Dec 1853, bapt. 13 Mar 1854 (Baptism, **St. Mary, Pro Cathedral Parish (RC)**)

Joseph Blundell (father):

Residence - 15 Elliott Place - March 13, 1854

- Joseph Blundell & Mary Ingham – 17 Feb 1748 (Marriage, **St. Bride Parish**)

  o Joseph Blundell – bapt. 13 Oct 1750 (Baptism, **St. Werburgh Parish**)

  o Anne Blundell – bapt. 4 Nov 1751 (Baptism, **St. Werburgh Parish**)

  o Joseph Blundell – bapt. 7 Aug 1755 (Baptism, **St. Werburgh Parish**)

  o Elizabeth Blundell – bapt. 23 Sep 1756 (Baptism, **St. Werburgh Parish**)

  o Joseph Blundell – bapt. 3 Nov 1757 (Baptism, **St. Werburgh Parish**)

  o Mary Blundell – bapt. 19 Nov 1758 (Baptism, **St. Werburgh Parish**), bur. 11 Jun 1765 (Burial, **St. Werburgh Parish**)

Mary Blundell (daughter):

Residence -Werburgh Street - before June 11, 1765

Age at Death - 6 years

Cause of Death - decay

  o Sarah Blundell – bapt. Apr 1760 (Baptism, **St. Werburgh Parish**)

  o Charles Blundell – bapt. 24 Apr 1761 (Baptism, **St. Werburgh Parish**)

  o Richard Blundell – bapt. 10 Oct 1762 (Baptism, **St. Werburgh Parish**)

  o Lydia Blundell – bapt. 13 Mar 1764 (Baptism, **St. Werburgh Parish**)

Hurst

o   Henry Blundell – bapt. 4 Feb 1767 (Baptism, **St. Werburgh Parish**)

Joseph Blundell (husband):

Residence - Werburgh Street - October 13, 1750

November 1, 1751

August 7, 1755

September 23, 1756

November 3, 1757

November 19, 1758

April 24, 1761

October 10, 1762

March 13, 1764

February 4, 1767

Occupation - Merchant - February 17, 1748

Blundell Surname Ireland: 1600s to 1900s

- Joseph Blundell & Unknown

  o Elizabeth Blundell & John Burke

Signatures:

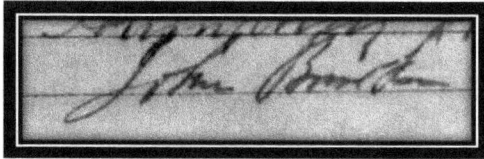

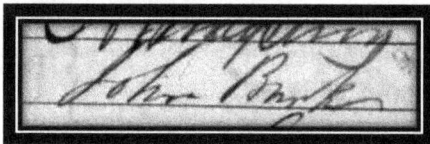

- James Edmund Burke – b. 1859, bapt. 1859 (Baptism, **St. Andrew Parish** (RC))

- Frederick William Burke – b. 1860, bapt. 1860 (Baptism, **St. Andrew Parish** (RC))

John Burke (father):

Residence - 17 D'Olier Street - 1859

1860

Hurst

o Frances Blundell & George Minchin – 20 Oct 1853 (Marriage, **St. Mark Parish**)

Signatures:

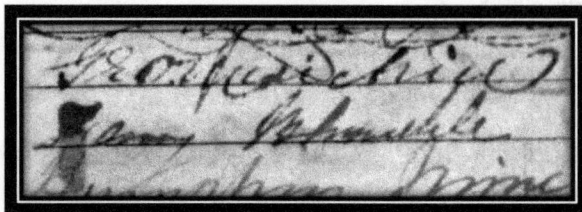

Frances Blundell (daughter):

Residence - 17 D'Olier Street - October 20, 1853

St. Mark Parish - October 20, 1853

George Minchin, son of Richard Charles Henry Minchin & Unknown (son-in-law):

Residence - 4 Ormond Terrace, Rathmines - October 20, 1853

Rathmines - October 20, 1853

Occupation - Gentleman - October 20, 1853

Richard Charles Henry Minchin (father):

Occupation - Clerk

Joseph Blundell (father):

   Occupation - Hotel Keeper

Wedding Witnesses:

Humphrey Minchin & John Burke

Signatures:

Hurst

○ Catherine Blundell & Samuel Spaight – 11 Oct 1859 (Marriage, **St. Mark Parish**)

Signatures:

Catherine Blundell (daughter):

Residence - 17 D'Olier Street - October 11, 1859

St. Mark Parish - October 11, 1859

Samuel Spaight, son of Thomas Spaight & Unknown (son-in-law):

Residence - 62 York Street Kingston - October 11, 1859

Monkstown - October 11, 1859

Occupation - Hotel Keeper - October 11, 1859

Thomas Spaight (father):

Occupation - Gentleman

Joseph Blundell (father):

   Occupation - Hotel Keeper

Wedding Witnesses:

Frederick Blundell & William Hawkins

Signatures:

- Matthew Frazer Blundell & Catherine Blundell

  o Catherine Blundell & Horace Reginald Waters – 5 Jun 1893 (Baptism, **St. Peter Parish**)

Signatures:

Hurst

Catherine Blundell (daughter):

    Residence - 11 Upper Pembroke Street & Kilrush - June 5, 1893

Horace Reginald Waters, son of Thomas Garrett Waters & Unknown (son-in-law):

    Residence - Edenderry King's County - June 5, 1893

    Occupation - Civil Engineer - June 5, 1893

Thomas Garrett Waters (father):

    Occupation - Engineer

Matthew Frazer Blundell (father):

    Occupation - Officer of Inland Revenue

Wedding Witnesses:

M. Williams & N. L. Waters

Signatures:

- Thomas Henry Blundell – b. 4 Oct 1863, bapt. 17 Jan 1864 (Baptism, **Rathmines Parish**)

Matthew Frazer Blundell (father):

    Residence - Dunville House - January 17, 1864

    Occupation - Excise Officer - January 17, 1864

        Officer of Inland Revenue

Blundell Surname Ireland: 1600s to 1900s

- Michael Blundell & Ellen Shiel

  - Robert Blundell – bapt. 10 Aug 1846 (Baptism, **St. Nicholas Parish** (RC))

- Michael Blundell & Ellen Shiel

  - Robert Blundell – bapt. 16 Nov 1846 (Baptism, **St. Nicholas Parish** (RC))

- Patrick Blundell & Anne Cavanagh – 19 Aug 1822 (Marriage, **St. Mark Parish**)

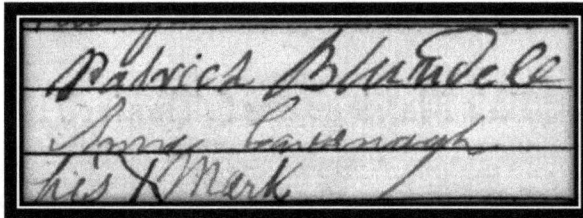

Signatures:

- Patrick Blundell & Sarah Jones – 8 Mar 1805 (Marriage, **St. Peter Parish**)

  - William Blundell – bapt. 14 Jul 1811 (Baptism, **St. Peter Parish**)

  - Sarah Blundell – b. 31 Oct 1813, bapt. 7 Nov 1813 (Baptism, **St. Peter Parish**)

Patrick Blundell (father):

Residence - Harcourt Street - July 14, 1811

- Peter Blundell & Elizabeth Unknown

  - Jane Blundell – bapt. 12 Jun 1808 (Baptism, **St. Peter Parish**)

  - Rachel Blundell – bapt. 13 May 1810 (Baptism, **St. Werburgh Parish**)

  - Charles Blundell – b. 1814, bapt. 10 Jul 1814 (Baptism, **St. James Parish**)

  - James Blundell – b. 1817, bapt. 25 Sep 1817 (Baptism, **St. James Parish**)

  - Joshua Thomas Blundell – b. 1820, bapt. 28 May 1820 (Baptism, **St. James Parish**)

Hurst

Peter Blundell (father):

Residence - Stephen Street - June 12, 1808

Canal Bridge - May 13, 1810

- Peter Blundell & Susan Blundell

  o Gaspero Blundell (daughter) – bapt. 14 Apr 1770 (Baptism, **St. Mary Parish**)

Peter Blundell (father):

Residence - Britain Street - April 14, 1770

- Ralph Blundell & Dorothy Unknown

  o Mary Blundell – bapt. 7 Feb 1737 (Baptism, **St. Audoen Parish**)

- Ralph Blundell & Jane Unknown

  o Daniel Blundell – bapt. 12 Dec 1724 (Baptism, **St. Audoen Parish**)

  o John Blundell – bapt. 8 Dec 1727 (Baptism, **St. Audoen Parish**)

  o Richard Blundell – bapt. 8 Mar 1731 (Baptism, **St. Audoen Parish**)

  o Anne Blundell – bapt. 19 Aug 1733 (Baptism, **St. Audoen Parish**)

- Richard Blundell & Anne Magrane

  o George Christopher Blundell – b. 1870, bapt. 1870 (Baptism, **St. Andrew Parish (RC)**)

Richard Blundell (father):

Residence - 7 Harmony Row - 1870

- Richard Blundell & Teresa Mahony – 29 Aug 1853 (Marriage, **St. Mary, Pro Cathedral Parish (RC)**)

- o Henry Christopher Blundell – b. 15 Apr 1855, bapt. 25 Apr 1855 (Baptism, **St. Michan Parish** (RC))

Richard Blundell (father):

Residence - 11 Wellington Street - April 25, 1855

- Richard Benson B. H. Blundell & Unknown
  - o Richard Blundell Hollinshead Blundell & Henrietta Frances Kirwan – 5 Jan 1865 (Marriage, **St. Stephen Parish**)

Signatures:

Richard Blundell Hollinshead Blundell (son):

Residence - Calvary Barracks, Manchester - January 5, 1865

Occupation - Captain 3rd King's Hussars - January 5, 1865

Henrietta Frances Kirwan, daughter of Richard Kirwan & Unknown (daughter-in-law):

Residence - 42 Upper Mount Street - January 5, 1865

Richard Kirwan (father):

Occupation - Esquire J P

Richard Benson B. H. Blundell (father):

Occupation - Esquire

Wedding Witnesses:

G. Howard Vyse & Agnes J. Kirwan

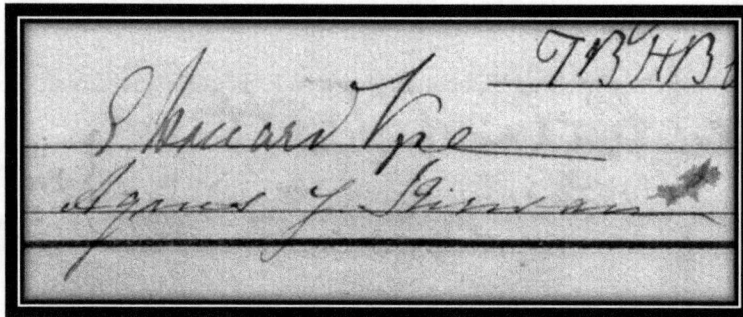

Signatures:

- Robert Blundell & Anne Blundell

  o Anne Blundell – Bapt. 15 Nov 1799 (Baptism, **St. Mary Parish**)

- Thomas Blundell & Catherine Blundell

  o Robert Charles Blundell – bapt. 17 Apr 1796 (Baptism, **St. Mary Parish**)

Thomas Blundell (father):

Residence - Henry Street - April 17, 1796

- Thomas Blundell & Elizabeth Blundell

  o Henry Blundell – bapt. 25 Sep 1814 (Baptism, **St. Mary Parish**)

  o Robert Blundell – bapt. 3 Mar 1816 (Baptism, **St. Mary Parish**)

Blundell Surname Ireland: 1600s to 1900s

- Thomas Blundell & Lydia Thomas – 21 Jul 1753 (Marriage, **St. John Parish**)

Thomas Blundell (husband):

   Occupation - Watchmaker

Lydia Thomas (wife):

   Occupation - Spinster

- Thomas Blundell & Margaret Blundell

   o   Thomas Henry Blundell – b. 12 Aug 1843, bapt. 20 Aug 1843 (Baptism, **Listowel Parish**)

- Thomas Henry Blundell & Elizabeth Blundell

   o   Thomas Joseph Blundell – bapt. 7 Mar 1813 (Baptism, **St. Werburgh Parish**)

Thomas Henry Blundell (father):

   Residence - Mary Street - March 7, 1813

- Unknown Blundell & Unknown

   o   Amelia Blundell

Signature:

- Unknown Blundell & Unknown

    o Anne Blundell

Signature:

- Unknown Blundell & Unknown

    o Charles Wilson Blundell

Signature:

- Unknown Blundell & Unknown

    o George Blundell

Signatures:

- Unknown Blundell & Unknown

    o Henry Blundell

Signature:

Blundell Surname Ireland: 1600s to 1900s

- Unknown Blundell & Unknown

  o John Blundell

Signature:

- Unknown Blundell & Unknown

  o Patrick Blundell

Signature:

- Unknown Blundell & Unknown

  o Robert Blundell

Signature:

- Walter Blundell & Margaret Freeman

  o George Blundell – b. 31 Jan 1870, bapt. 4 Feb 1870 (Baptism, **St. Nicholas Parish (RC)**)

Walter Blundell (father):

Residence - 10 Peter's Row - February 4, 1870

Hurst

- William Blundell & Adela Blundell

  o William George Blundell – b. 7 Jan 1862, bapt. 2 Feb 1863 (Baptism, **Portobello Barracks Parish**)

William Blundell (father):

Residence - Ship Street Barracks - February 2, 1863

Occupation - Sergeant 36th Royal Horse Artillery - February 2, 1863

- William Blundell & Anne Blundell

  o George Blundell – bapt. 19 May 1670 (Baptism, **St. Michan Parish**)

William Blundell (father):

Occupation - Esquire - May 19, 1670

- William Blundell & Gertrude King – 7 Oct 1794 (Marriage, **St. Mary Parish**)

  o Dixie Blundell (son) – bapt. 17 Jul 1799 (Baptism, **St. Mary Parish**)

  o Mary Blundell – b. 10 Aug 1801, bapt. 19 Aug 1801 (Baptism, **St. Mary Parish**)

  o Elizabeth Blundell – bapt. 20 Jul 1803 (Baptism, **St. Mary Parish**)

  o Robert Blundell – bapt. 20 Jun 1806 (Baptism, **St. Mary Parish**)

  o Gertrude Blundell – bapt. 2 Mar 1808 (Baptism, **St. Mary Parish**)

William Blundell (father):

Occupation - Curate, St. Mary's - July 17, 1799

Professional Title - Reverend

Blundell Surname Ireland: 1600s to 1900s

- William Blundell & Lucy Blundell

  - William Blundell – b. 15 Aug 1841, bapt. 10 Sep 1841 (Baptism, **St. Mary Parish**)

William Blundell (father):

   Residence - Co. Kilkenny - September 10, 1841

   Occupation - Farmer - September 10, 1841

- William Blundell & Lydia Blundell

  - John Blundell – bapt. 13 Sep 1795 (Baptism, **St. Mary Parish**)

- William Blundell & Unknown

  - Elizabeth Blundell – bapt. 2 Jun 1627 (Baptism, **St. John Parish**)

- William Blundell & Unknown

  - Mary Blundell & William Joynt – 6 Jun 1859 (Marriage, **St. Peter Parish**)

Signatures:

Mary Blundell (daughter):

   Residence - 10 Cambridge Terrace Rathgar - June 6, 1859

William Joynt, son of Thomas Joynt & Unknown (son-in-law):

   Residence - 2 Bengal Terrace Finglas, Glasnevin Parish - June 6, 1859

   Occupation - Gentleman - June 6, 1859

Hurst

Thomas Joynt (father):

Occupation - Gentleman

William Blundell (father):

Occupation - Watchmaker

Wedding Witnesses:

John Felton & Charles A. Taylor

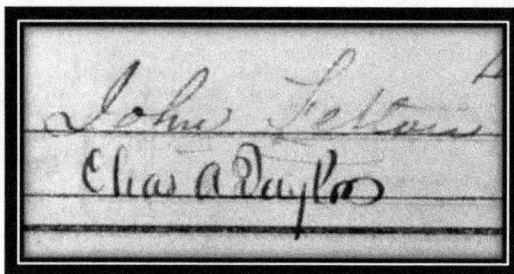

Signatures:

- William James Blundell & Mary Anne Teresa Blundell

  o Angelina Blundell – b. 25 Sep 1895, bapt. 20 Oct 1895 (Baptism, **Ballymacelligott & Ballyseedy Parish**)

  o William John Blundell – b. 10 Dec 1897, bapt. 17 Apr 1898 (Baptism, **Killehenney Parish**)

  o Charles Henry Blundell – b. 4 May 1900, bapt. 4 Oct 1900 (Baptism, **Tralee Parish**)

  o Archibald C. Blundell – b. 12 Jun 1901, bapt. 15 Oct 1901 (Baptism, **Tralee Parish**)

  o Mabel C. Blundell – b. 19 Oct 1902, bapt. 8 Jul 1903 (Baptism, **Tralee Parish**)

  o Harriet E. Blundell – b. 26 Sep 1908, bapt. 16 Oct 1908 (Baptism, **Tralee Parish**)

  o Olive Frances Blundell – b. 20 Aug 1909, bapt. 29 Oct 1909 (Baptism, **Tralee Parish**)

Blundell Surname Ireland: 1600s to 1900s

William James Blundell (father):

Residence - Shanavalla Barrack - October 20, 1895

Ballybunion - April 17, 1898

Tralee - October 4, 1900

October 15, 1901

July 8, 1903

October 29, 1909

Almshouse - October 16, 1908

Occupation - Constable in R. I. C. - October 20, 1895

April 17, 1898

October 15, 1901

R. I. C. - October 4, 1900

July 8, 1903

Sexton - October 16, 1908

October 29, 1909

Individual Baptisms/Births

- Anne Blundell – bapt. 15 Nov 1676 (Baptism, **St. Peter Parish**)

- Lewis Nicholas Blundell – bapt. 13 Sep 1827 (Baptism, **St. Mary Parish**)

- Mary Elizabeth Blundell – b. 2 Mar 1863, bapt. 8 Mar 1863 (Baptism, **Rotunda Chapel Parish**)

- Susan Jane Mary Blundell – b. 28 May 1874 (Baptism, **Kinsale Parish (RC)**)

Individual Burials

- Anne Blundell – bur. 6 Sep 1776 (Burial, **St. James Parish**)

Anne Blundell (deceased):

> Residence - Thomas Street - before September 6, 1776

- Anne Blundell – bur. 9 Feb 1813 (Burial, **St. James Parish**)

Anne Blundell (deceased):

> Residence - Dig Street - before February 9, 1813

- Anne Blundell – b. 1823, d. 30 Apr 1856, bur. 1856 (Burial, **St. Peter Parish**)

Anne Blundell (deceased):

> Residence - 3 Lower Clanbrassil Street - April 30, 1856

> Age at Death - 33 years

- Anne Blundell – b. 1788, bur. 9 Dec 1864 (Burial, **St. George Parish**)

Anne Blundell (deceased):

> Residence - Servant's Asylum Lower Dorset Street - before December 9, 1864

> Age at Death - 76 years

- Charles Blundell – b. 1851, d. 7 Jul 1863 (Burial, **St. James Parish**)

Hurst

Charles Blundell (deceased):

Residence - Steven's Hospital - July 7, 1863

Age at Death - 12 years

- H. L. Blundell – bur. 26 Mar 1807 (Burial, **Glasnevin Parish**)

- Henry Blundell – bur. 3 Nov 1674 (Burial, **St. Peter Parish**)

- John Blundell – b. 1780, bur. 4 Feb 1832 (Burial, **St. Peter Parish**)

John Blundell (deceased):

Residence - Kevin Street - before February 4, 1832

Age at Death - 52 years

- Martha Jane Blundell – b. 1852, d. 30 Jul 1853, bur. 1853 (Burial, **St. Peter Parish**)

Martha Jane Blundell (deceased):

Residence - Malpas Street - July 30, 1853

Age at Death - 1 year

- Mary Blundell – b. 1786, bur. 20 Aug 1831 (Burial, **St. George Parish**)

Mary Blundell (deceased):

Residence - Dorset Street - before August 20, 1831

Age at Death - 45 years

Blundell Surname Ireland: 1600s to 1900s

- Mary Blundell – b. 1855, d. 18 Mar 1878, bur. 1878 (Burial, **St. James Parish**)

Mary Blundell (deceased):

Residence - South Dublin Union - March 18, 1878

Age at Death - 23 years

- Mary Anne Blundell – bur. 6 Feb 1804 (Burial, **St. Paul Parish**)

- Mary Anne Blundell – b. 1768, bur. 21 Sep 1841 (Burial, **St. Mary Parish**)

Mary Anne Blundell (deceased):

Residence - Drumcondra - before September 21, 1841

Age at Death - 73 years

- Thomas Blundell – bur. 13 Oct 1726 (Burial, **St. Paul Parish**)

- Thomas Blundell – bur. 8 Apr 1804 (Burial, **St. Paul Parish**)

- Unknown Blundell (Mrs.) – bur. 15 Jul 1717 (Burial, **St. Patirck Parish**)

Church Register Entry:

"[Blank] Blondell late wife of [Blank] Blondell interred in ye Vicars Bawne."

- Walter Blundell – bur. 1 Mar 1709 (Burial, **St. Nicholas Without Parish**)

Walter Blundell (deceased):

Residence - Patrick Street - before March 1, 1709

Individual Marriages

- Alice Blundell & Edward Blackburn (B l a c k b u r n) – 16 Sep 1752 (Marriage, **St. John Parish**)

Edward Blackburn (husband):

Occupation - Merchant - September 16, 1752

- Anne Blundell & Gulielmo Eskins

  o Amelia Eskins – bapt. 5 Feb 1826 (Baptism, **St. Michan Parish (RC)**)

- Anne Blundell & John Reilly – 4 Sep 1811 (Marriage, **St. Michan Parish (RC)**)

  o James Reilly – bapt. 5 Sep 1819 (Baptism, **St. Michan Parish (RC)**)

- Anne Blundell & Thomas Roney – 26 Dec 1827 (Marriage, **St. Michan Parish (RC)**)

- Bridget Blundell & Patrick Hannon

  o Bridget Hannon – b. 1883, bapt. 1883 (Baptism, **St. Andrew Parish (RC)**)

Patrick Hannon (father):

Residence - 15 Stephen's Lane - 1883

- Catherine Blundell & Terence O'Rielly – 25 Mar 1820 (Marriage, **St. Andrew Parish (RC)**)

- Dorothea Blundell & Sterne (S t e r n e) Tighe – 28 Feb 1716 (Marriage, **St. Michan Parish**)

Sterne Tighe (husband):

Occupation - Merchant - February 28, 1716

Blundell Surname Ireland: 1600s to 1900s

- Elizabeth Blundell & Edward Byrne (B y r n e) – 1 Jan 1845 (Marriage, **St. Mark Parish**) (Marriage, **St. Andrew Parish** (RC))

Signatures:

Elizabeth Blundell (wife):

   Residence - **St. Mark Parish** - January 1, 1845

Edward Byrne (husband):

   Residence - **St. Peter's Parish** - January 1, 1845

Wedding Witnesses:

Joseph Blundell & Thomas Byrne

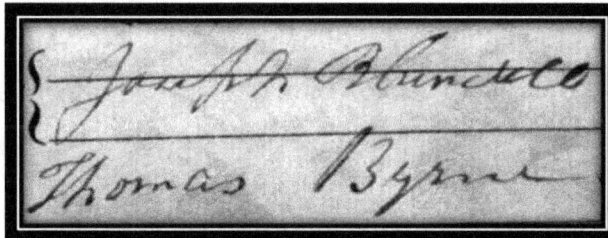

Signatures:

- Elizabeth Blundell & Edward Mitchell – 30 Nov 1799 (Marriage, **St. Mary Parish**)

Edward Mitchell (husband):

   Occupation - Esquire - November 30, 1799

Hurst

- Elizabeth Blundell & Edward Reynolds – 27 Jul 1819 (Marriage, St. Mary, Pro Cathedral Parish (RC))

- Elizabeth Blundell & Thomas Prentice – 24 Dec 1795 (Marriage, St. Michan Parish)

Elizabeth Blundell (wife):

Residence - St. Michan's Parish - December 24, 1795

Thomas Prentice (husband):

Residence - City of Dublin - December 24, 1794

Occupation - Merchant - December 24, 1794

- Elizabeth Blundell & William Insley – 10 Jun 1675 (Marriage, St. Bride Parish)

- Jane Blundell & John Crofton – 28 Sep 1811 (Marriage, St. George Parish)

John Crofton (husband):

Occupation - Gentleman - September 28, 1811

- Mary Blundell & John Manwarring Uniac – 4 Aug 1794 (Marriage, St. Mary Parish)

John Manwarring Uniac (husband):

Occupation - Esquire - August 4, 1794

- Mary Blundell & Robert Thornton (T h o r n t o n) – 28 Oct 1656 (Marriage, St. John Parish)

- Mary Blundell & Thomas Gunnings – 11 Jan 1657 (Marriage, St. Bride Parish)

- Mary Anne Blundell & William McCowen – 2 Aug 1829 (Marriage, Dingle Parish)

Blundell Surname Ireland: 1600s to 1900s

Mary Anne Blundell (wife):

    Residence - Dingle - August 2, 1829

William McCowen (husband):

    Residence - Dingle - August 2, 1829

Name Variations

Includes Latin and Abbreviated forms of names found in the original documents.

Abigail = Abigale, Abigall

Anne = Ann, Anna, Annae

Bartholomew = Barth, Bartholmeus, Bartholomeo

Bridget = Birgis, Brigid, Brigida, Bridgit

Catherine = Catharine, Catharina, Catharinae, Catherina, Cath, Catha, Cathae, Cathe, Cathn, Kate

Charles = Carolus, Charls, Chas

Christopher = Christoph

Daniel = Danielem, Danielis

Edmund = Edmond

Edward = Ed, Edwd

Eleanor = Eleo, Eleonora, Elinor, Ellenor

Elizabeth = Betty, Elisa, Elisabeth, Eliz, Eliza, Elizab, Elizh, Elizth

Ellen = Elena, Ellena

Emily = Emilia

Esther = Essie, Ester

Francis = Fransicum

George = Geo, Georg, Georgius

Grace = Gratiae

Gulielmo = Guil, Guillelmi, Gulielmum, Guillelmus, Gulmi

Blundell Surname Ireland: 1600s to 1900s

Helen = Helena

Honor = Hanora, Honora

James = Jacobi, Jacobus, Jas

Jane = Joanna

Jeanne = Jeannae, Joannae

Joan = Johanna, Joney

John = Jno, Joannem, Joannes, Johannis

Joseph = Jos

Juliana = Julian

Leticia = Letitia, Lettice, Letticia

Lewis = Louis

Luke = Lucas

Margaret = Margarita, Margaritae, Margeret, Marget, Margt

Martha = Marthae

Mary = Maria, My

Mary Anne = Marianna, Marianne, Maryanne

Michael = Michaelis, Michl

Patrick = Pat, Patt, Patk, Patricii, Patricius

Peter = Petri

Richard = Ricardi, Ricardus, Rich, Richd

Robert = Roberti

Rose = Rosa, Rosae

Thomas = Thom, Thomae, Thoms, Thos, Ths

Timothy = Timotheus, Timy

William = Wil, Will, Willm, Wm

Notes

Notes

Notes

Notes

Notes

Notes

Index

A

Adams
Jane 9

B

Barry
Sarah 5
Blackburn
Edward 40
Blundell
Amelia 29
Anne 30
Baptims
Martha
1865 Jan 17 10
Baptisms
Albert
1881 Mar 30 13
Amelia
1863 Jan 12 6
Amelia Caroline
1853 May 1 8
Amelia Jane
1873 Sep 15 6
Andrew
1835 Dec 11 1
1866 May 18 5
Angelina
1895 Oct 20 34

Anne
1676 Nov 15 36
1733 Aug 19 26
1751 Nov 4 17
1799 Nov 15 28
1824 Oct 10 16
1834 Aug 18 1
Archibald C.
1901 Oct 15 34
Charles
1684 Jan 17 4
1761 Apr 24 17
1814 Jul 10 25
Charles Henry
1900 Oct 4 34
Daniel
1724 Dec 12 26
Dixie
1799 Jul 17 32
Dorothy
1699 Jun 22 3
Elizabeth
1627 Jun 2 33
1756 Sep 23 17
1803 Jul 20 32
1821 Sep 16 16
Elizabeth Sibela
1695 Jul 21 3
Elizabeth Teresa
1845 Oct 27 1
Gaspero
1770 Apr 14 26
George
1670 32
1775 Jan 17 4
1788 Mar 26 8

52

Blundell Surname Ireland: 1600s to 1900s

Blundell Surname Ireland: 1600s to 1900s

W

Wade

About The Author

Donovan Hurst graduated from San Diego State University with a Bachelor of Arts in the major field of studies of History and a minor in the field of studies of Anthropology. He is a current member of The General Society of Mayflower Descendants and has been conducting genealogical research for over 10 years tracing back his ancestors to their ancestral homelands in Denmark, England, France, Germany, Ireland, Norway, and Scotland.